I will be happy once _____ happens

E. K. Christopher

Copyright © 2017 E.K. Christopher

All rights reserved.

ISBN: 0998744603
ISBN-13: 978-0998744605

DEDICATION

To all of those who feel empty and lost. We enter into this world with no definitive truth to guide us, which is why life is so frustrating and confusing. I wrote this book for all of you, so that we can work together in finding clarity and peace.

CONTENTS

	Preface	i
1	Fill in the Blank	1
2	The Void	5
3	Fantasy World	11
4	Resistance	17
5	The Mirage	23
6	Thoughts	29
7	Joy Shower	35
8	The Present Moment	43
9	Retrain Your Mind	47

PREFACE

I am not a doctor or any other type of professional who would normally write a book such as this. I am a regular person, just like you. I wrote this book with myself in mind from a few years ago. At that time in my life, I was highly skeptical of books like this one, just as many of you are today. I inadvertently stumbled upon knowledge that changed the way I view the world and knew I had to find a more effective way of sharing it with others. This book is the result of those efforts.

You will notice the format is not like most books. This book is very brief and direct because I don't believe in making you sift through layers of fluff in order to get to the point. I believe the brevity is necessary because when most of us read, we *see* the words on the page, but rarely take the effort to fully interpret the meaning behind them. Using a limited number of words encourages you to pause and reflect on the message instead of allowing it to pass by.

Because it is so short, it is possible to read the entire thing in under an hour. However, if you want to get the most out of it, I suggest you do not rush through it. Each sentence is meant to be carefully contemplated and mentally digested before moving on. Spend as much time as you need to with each chapter before moving on to the next, even if it means a few weeks. This is a small book, but it may take months to effectively get through and master. I hope it helps you find some clarity in your life.

1
FILL IN THE BLANK

Belief #1:
"I will be happy once _____ happens."

Many of us go through life on autopilot, not really living at all.

We "kill time" waiting for life to happen to us.

We believe happiness is something off in the future, which we must find or wait for.

We believe if we do everything on our checklist and acquire everything we want, then we will arrive at a place called happiness.

We believe happiness is caused by factors from the outside world.

We believe happiness is a few brief moments in time, which aren't meant to last.

We wait for happiness to happen to us.

> *Notice moments when you are waiting for something to make you happy.*

2
THE VOID

Belief #2:
"Possessions and people make me feel happy."

Sometimes we feel empty, discontent, or as if there is a void inside of us that we must fill in order to be happy.

We feel as if we need to find something that will complete us.

We view life as a mountain we must struggle to climb. We believe once we've made it to the top (when we've arranged everything how we want it to be, and accumulated everything we want), we will live happily ever after on the peak of bliss.

We feel we must do or use something in order to create happiness.

In an attempt to complete ourselves, we use things from the outside world like material possessions and attention/acceptance from other people. Examples include: money, car, house, jewelry, clothes, appearance, electronic gadgets, likes/followers on social media, and much, much more.

> ➤ *How do you feel when you buy a new pair of shoes, receive a text message, or someone likes your photo on social media?*

Our current perception of life: we are in a constant state of unhappiness, emptiness, or unease. We experience temporary flashes of happiness, brought about by people, things, and situations. In other words:

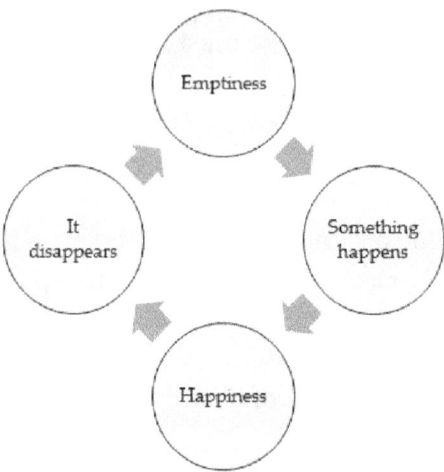

We are constantly searching for temporary moments of happiness. We always want something else or wait for something better than what we currently have.

These things give us temporary relief, but the emptiness and urge for more always returns.

We believe if we can just collect enough of these moments, we will finally become happy.

If you are not happy with what you currently have, will adding more really make a difference?

> *Notice the sensation of temporary happiness brought about by people and things.*

3
FANTASY WORLD

Belief #3:
"My beliefs are right and yours are wrong."

We try to find our way to happiness by collecting material possessions, people, and circumstances. We also attempt to find or create happiness within our mental world as well.

We create a "fantasy world" inside of our mind, which is comprised of our beliefs, likes/dislikes, and general idea of how the world functions. Most of us do this without even realizing it.

This "fantasy world" identifies who we believe we are and is our primary sense of self.

It is created by the things we experience throughout our life. We are essentially a collection of every interaction we have ever had.

We believe our world-view is correct because it is all we have ever experienced. We are hesitant to experience, or even consider, anything foreign to what we are familiar with.

> *Creatures of habit*

We prefer things remain predictable, familiar, and safe. We prefer for the outside world to match the fantasy inside our head.

We constantly compare reality to the fantasy we have built inside our mind, whether we realize it or not.

We want the outside world, including the behavior of others, to suit us.

This is a problem because not everyone in the world has walked the same path in life as we have. Not everyone feels and thinks like we do.

Everyone has a distinct fantasy inside his or her head and wants the outside world match it, just like you do.

Because there are so many different world-views out there, you will never be able to change every situation or person to be exactly how you want it to be.

You have no control over how other people think, feel, or behave.

The only person whose thoughts, feelings, and actions you have control over are your own.

You can only control yourself. Focus on your life and your actions.

> ➢ *How do we recognize when we are guilty of living in our "fantasy world?"*

Complaining, either mentally or verbally, is our way of pointing out differences between our fantasy (how we want the world to be) and reality (how the world actually is.)

When we notice something we do not like, we complain or argue because we want it to match the fantasy inside our head. Examples include: getting offended by someone's words or behavior, disagreements over politics or religion, or getting involved in a physical fight.

Feeling uncomfortable or defensive is a sign that something new is presenting itself to you. This is a chance to learn and grow. Instead of sticking with what you are used to, try to step outside of your comfort zone and experience something new.

Notice how many times you complain, or feel like complaining, throughout the day.

4
RESISTANCE

Belief #4:
"I must arrange my life exactly how I want it to be."

We constantly work to uphold the fantasy inside of our head.

We want to keep everything in our life the same and predictable.

> *Everything changes*

There is one problem with wanting things to remain predictable and trying to permanently define the world around us: nothing in the world is permanent. Everything is in a constant state of change.

Everything arises, changes, and decays.

Even as you sit there, reading these words, your body is in a constant state of change; cells are dying, blood is pumping, dead skin cells fall off your body, etc.

Your body is not the same now as it was at 5 years old; it is now comprised of entirely new cells and looks completely different.

Most of life's changes happen slowly; therefore, we do not notice as they happen. For example, we do not notice as hair or trees grow.

This does not only happen physically, it is mental and emotional as well.

Every experience you have in life changes you in some way, even if you do not realize it at the time.

Because of impermanence, no situation or person will remain the same forever.

Most of the things we attach our happiness to are impermanent.

> *"No man ever steps in the same river twice, for it is not the same river and he is not the same man." –Heraclitus*

> ➢ *Resisting reality*

Resisting the natural changes in life is what causes us to suffer.

Pain and frustration occur by either holding on to the past and resisting the move forward, or by resisting reality because you are focused on the fantasy inside of your mind.

Imagine trying to keep paper plates on a picnic table during a hurricane. It will result in never-ending frustration because the plates will continue to blow away. This is similar to the frustration we feel when trying to arrange life according to the fantasy inside of our head. Life continues to move forward just as the wind of the hurricane continues to blow.

Many relationships have problems because of impermanence. We want our partner to remain how he or she was at the beginning of the relationship.

Most airports have moving walkways, which look like a flat escalator, where walkers stand in place and it takes them where they need to go. Life is supposed to be like this moving walkway, where we continuously move forward at a steady pace.

This is not how many of us currently live. We tend to hold on to how things currently are or used to be, which keeps us in place, in a state of resistance, not progressing forward.

We hold on to moments in time when we were happy and resist moving forward.

Life is not one single moment that you get to and then stay there until you die. It is constant change.

We must continue to evolve. We must flow naturally

through life, embracing its natural changes, instead of holding on to fond moments.

Instead of getting upset when things do not go according to our fantasy, we need to learn to accept things how they are.

Getting angry, upset, or frustrated will not change the situation and it will not make it un-happen. Accept it and move on.

Live life how it is, instead of how you *want* it to be.

> ➢ *Does this mean I must just sit back and accept it when something bad is happening?*

No, it doesn't. It only means you must not get angry or upset at the situation. It happened, and no amount of crying or complaining will change that. If you *must* do something in response to it, do it. If not, don't dwell on it. Move on.

When you feel a bad emotion, it is because you are resisting how things are. In other words, you are living inside your fantasy rather than reality.

Notice your bad emotions.
They are a sign of resistance.

5
THE MIRAGE

Belief #5:
"My emotions are caused by people and situations. I have no control over how I feel."

What is an emotion?

We believe an emotion is something felt as the result of the circumstances or situations we experience.

Right now, this is our general understanding of emotions:

He calls me a name → I feel sad or angry → He made me feel this way
OR
The one I love walks into the room → I feel happy or excited → He made me feel this way

A mirage is an illusion that appears to be real but is not. The scenarios listed above are examples of a mirage, which blinds many of us.

The mirage is that we believe people, possessions, and situations create the way we feel.

The truth is, an emotion is *really* our body's response to what is going on inside of our mind.

In other words: **Our thoughts create our emotions.**

Here is what is *really* happening:

He calls me a name → I have an angry or sad thought in response → I feel sad or angry → I made myself feel this way

Right now, we believe the event itself causes our feelings about it; however, it is really what we *tell ourselves* about the event.

Think of there as being two buttons in your mind: a "happy thought button" and a "bad thought button."

When something happens, you push one of these buttons (most of the time without realizing it), and an emotion is created and dispensed into your body.
For example, in traffic when someone cuts you off:

THOUGHT 1: I don't like being cut off. What a jerk! I can't believe he did that!
EMOTION 1: Anger or hostility.
Or
THOUGHT 2: It's ok, it's not like it caused an accident. I will still get there on time.
EMOTION 2: Peace and calmness.

In the previous example, it was the exact same situation, yet there were two different reactions and two different emotions. This demonstrates that just because someone cuts you off, you don't *have* to become angry, you *choose* to become angry.

> *How exactly do "thought buttons" work?*

Imagine you go to buy a soda. At the soda fountain, if you push the grape button, grape-flavored soda will dispense into your cup. If you push the cherry button, you will get cherry.

The way we currently live is like this: we walk up to the fountain for a grape soda. However, we push the cherry button instead of the grape button. We do not understand why we did not receive grape. Instead of realizing *we* are the one who pushed the cherry button, we blame it on the person, object, or situation we are looking at.

We do the same thing with our emotions as well. We tend to blame others for our feelings and circumstances.

YOU create how you feel, not situations, people, or objects.

You have a choice in how you respond to situations. You can control the thoughts you have. You can choose the emotions you create.

Our mind has a *negative* reaction → Produces a *negative* emotion
Our mind has a *positive* reaction → Creates a *positive* emotion

"Holding on to anger is like drinking poison and expecting the other person to die." -Aristotle

Nobody has the power to reach inside of you and create your thoughts.
Nobody has the power to reach inside of you and create your emotions.

"Men are disturbed not by things that happen, but by their opinions of the things that happen." –Epictetus

> ➢ Does this mean I must sit here and watch every single thought I have to avoid feeling bad?

No, thankfully this is not necessary:

Notice when you have a bad feeling. It is the sign of a bad thought. Take a look at the thought that caused it.

6
THOUGHTS

Belief #6: "It is normal to become preoccupied with thoughts of the past and future."

Because thoughts cause our emotions, wouldn't it be beneficial to see what is really going on inside of our mind?

We have constant chatter going on inside of our mind. We have an endless stream of thoughts that, most of the time, we aren't even aware of.

> *Most of our thoughts are concentrated on the past and future*

The past: reliving our memories over and over again. Either thinking about how we wish we were still there, or how we wish it had turned out.

The future: fantasizing about, and anticipating how, we want things to be. Fear and worry are caused by thinking about the future.

Memories and fantasies cause emotions too. Imagine sitting in a relaxing bubble bath while thinking about a stressful moment from earlier that day. The bubble bath suddenly isn't so relaxing, is it?

Notice how many times you relive the past or fantasize about the future.

> *How can we become aware of what's going on inside our mind?*

The following exercise will help you become more aware of the chatter inside of your mind:

The exercise goes like this: Find a quiet, comfortable spot, away from any distractions. Next, picture a flower in your mind, any kind of flower, it doesn't matter. Then take a deep breath, relax, close your eyes, and focus on the flower (or the word flower) for a couple of minutes. That's it.

Some of you may be thinking, "What is the point of this? Sit there thinking about a flower? What the heck is that supposed to accomplish?" What you are going to be surprised to find is how hard it is to keep yourself focused on this one object or word for just a few minutes. You will be sitting there thinking, "Flower, flower, flower….." Then, before you know it, you will realize you are thinking about what to eat for dinner. "What am I doing? Where did *that* come from?" You don't even know how long you were thinking about dinner. It could have been 30 seconds or more before you realized that you weren't thinking about the flower anymore. All you need to do at this point is get back to the flower. The point is not to become upset with yourself or frustrated when you find your mind wandering. You shouldn't think, "I can't stay focused! This isn't working! I'm not going to do this anymore." *The fact that you realize you aren't staying focused, means it is working*. Just catch yourself being unfocused, and get back to the flower. That's it. The act of drawing attention to the chatter helps limit the amount of it in the future.

We do not realize how many thoughts go through our mind on a daily basis. During this two-minute period, you will catch yourself having at least a dozen stray thoughts, if not more. If you have this many thoughts in only two minutes, when you are actually trying to focus, imagine how many thoughts you have during a normal day, surrounded by endless stimulation and distraction.

> *What kinds of thoughts are running around up there?*

Not only do we reminisce and fantasize, but our mind also continuously judges people and events, labeling things as good or bad.

We are constantly evaluating if we like things or not, and deciding how things *should* be.

Each experience we have, no matter how big or small, creates a flurry of judgments within our mind.

Notice when you mentally label something good/bad or right/wrong.

7
JOY SHOWER

Belief #7: "Unhappiness is our normal state of being, temporarily relieved by short moments of happiness."

Earlier, we discussed how we believe happiness is caused by factors from the outside world and how we chase temporary moments of happiness:

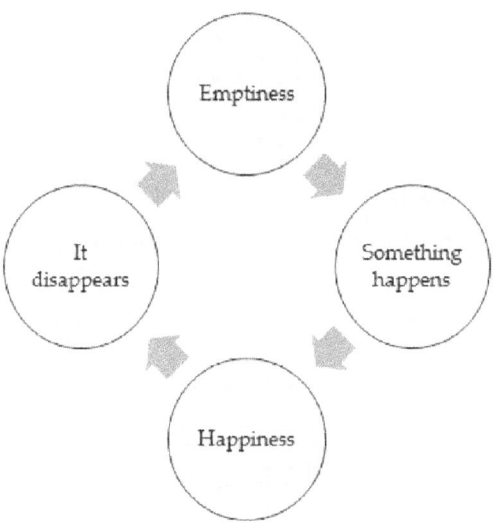

<u>Right now we believe</u>: **unhappiness** is permanent, obscured by temporary moments of happiness.

<u>Reality</u>: **happiness** is permanent, obscured by temporary moments of unhappiness.

Think of all the times you feel the "temporary" fulfillment you think of as happiness.

Examples include: buying new things, being noticed and accepted by others, likes and follows on social media, watching television or movies, playing video games, etc.

> *What is this "temporary moment of happiness" and how do we stay there permanently?*

Think of happiness as being a shower of water, which is always running and available to us.

When we are underneath the "shower," we feel happy. When we step outside of it, we feel unhappy.

Up until now, we have been taught that we must run around and arrange the outside world to our liking. We have been taught we must DO things and WAIT for happiness to be *given* to us.

Each time we try to create or chase happiness, we are actually *stepping outside of the shower*, which prevents us from feeling happiness. If we just stay where we are (metaphorically), we will remain happy, without interruption.

As we run around arranging our life, there are times

when we accidently pass underneath the shower. Instead of recognizing the true reason for this sudden jolt of happiness, we mistakenly believe it is caused by the object or person we are looking at. Objects and people do not cause it, we do.

How do we cause it?

Remember the lesson from earlier: **our thoughts create our emotions.** This includes happiness.

> *What is this metaphorical "joy shower" in real life?*

When your attention is not preoccupied by the past, future, and everything else, but instead focused on the present moment, you feel happy or content. You can only stand under the "joy shower" during the present moment.

When you are…
Staring at your phone: you are focused on what's in front of you.
Listening to music: you are focused on what's in front of you.
Watching TV or a movie: you are focused on what's in front of you.
Dancing: you are focusing on the present moment.
Having sex: you are focused on what's in front of you.

If you are truly focused on those things, with your mind not interfering, you feel happy, right?

During the previously mentioned moments, you are unknowingly standing underneath the joy shower (in the present moment) and feel happy; however, **you believe who or what you are looking at is the cause of the sensation.** *You are being fooled by the mirage.*

When you experience the sensation known as "love" this is actually the joy shower. The person you are "in love with" or "makes you feel this way" is just a distraction for your mind. You are focused on the person instead of your mind, which places you underneath the joy shower.

People say that the birth of your first child is the most amazing feeling in the world…. I wonder why?

You can feel this sensation whenever you want to, 24/7. You just have to decide to stand underneath the joy shower.

> *Not focused on the present moment*

When you are…
At work or school: you are thinking about being somewhere else.
Driving: you are thinking about being somewhere else.
Doing the dishes or laundry: you are thinking about doing something else.
Are you happy during these moments?

When our mind gets in the way, we slip out of the present moment and feel unhappy.

Notice moments when you feel happy. Examine whether or not it occurs because you have temporarily quieted your mind and are actually living in the present moment

8
THE PRESENT MOMENT

Belief #8:
"The current moment is not important. I must look ahead to what is next or remember what has already happened."

We are in the present moment when **our mind is quiet** and we are not fanaticizing or reminiscing.

Right now our mind would rather focus on anything except what is right in front of us. We do not believe the present moment is important.

Our mind is always thinking about the next event, party, or concert, and ignoring right now.

When we ignore the small and seemingly insignificant moments, we will always be looking for something more. Our entire life passes us by, while we **wait** for something else to happen.

We will feel as unfulfilled at the next event as we do right now.

Life is not about the big moments we plan for, the moments in between are what life is all about. **This moment, right now,** *is* **life.**

Try these exercises to practice staying in the present moment:

- Practice paying attention to your breathing. Focus on the air as you inhale and exhale.

- Take a quiet walk by yourself without your cell phone or any music playing. Clear your mind and try to focus on the entire experience of the walk. Notice the trees, birds, and wind as it blows.
  To help stay focused, try to spot all the letters of the alphabet in order on items around you as you pass them. This will help you stay focused on what is in front of you instead of what is inside your mind.

- Try to break any repetitive routines you may have. Change your daily routine in as many ways as you can.

Notice how you *feel* as you do these exercises. This will tell you if it is working.

During these exercises, it is important to not allow your mind to <u>reminisce</u>, <u>fanaticize</u>, or <u>complain</u>. These thoughts take you out of the present moment.

9
RETRAIN YOUR MIND

You might feel inspired right now, but once you put this book down you are going to forget everything you have learned. Your ideas about life been a part of you since you were young. You have spent your entire life engraining a certain world-view into your mind; right now it is almost second-nature. If you want to change the way you view the world, you must work to **retrain your mind** in order to perceive things differently. This is not a simple task, and it cannot be accomplished overnight. It will take a lot of repetition, determination, and hard work.

This will be especially difficult because most people you come into contact with are not aware of these ideas; therefore, others will continue to unconsciously pull you into the old ways of thinking and behaving. With almost every experience you have, you risk getting pulled out of the "Joy Shower." Just like when you tried to focus on the flower for two minutes, once you venture out into the real world, your mind will not stay focused and you will forget everything you have read here. To avoid this, you must continue to remind yourself of these ideas every day until they become second-nature if you truly wish to change your life.

Ever-lasting change is similar to losing weight. Many of us try the fad diets or pills, hoping we will wake up one morning with our ideal body; however, it does not work this way. If you really want to lose weight, you must put in the hard work of diet and exercise. It cannot and will not happen overnight, and no one else can do it for you. The same is true for the lessons presented in this book. You cannot expect to read this book and wake up a brand-new person, with your life changed forever. You must put in the hard work of *retraining your mind*. You can read all of the books and go to all of the lectures you want to, but nothing will change until you actively explore your mind and make the necessary changes.

Once you venture out into the real world, you must remember that other people have not read this book. Most of them are unaware of their thoughts, feelings, and motivations. You should not allow their behavior to discourage you; they are not aware of what they are doing. Do not allow the unconscious acts of others to take away your peace.

If you sincerely hope to prevent the outside world erasing your new understanding of life, you must use **repetition** to remind yourself of these lessons every day.

Things to continuously remind yourself of:

Non-Attachment: Do not obtain your self-worth or happiness from possessions, people, or ideas.

Non-Resistance (acceptance): No complaining. Accept things how they are. Remember, life is a continuous cycle of change.

Non-Judgement: Do not label yourself or compare yourself to others.

Mindfulness: Watch your thoughts and emotions in order to stay in the present moment and under the "Joy Shower."

Solitude: Schedule some quiet and peaceful "me time." This allows you to focus on quieting your mind without the interference of others. This is most effective if done outside and without any distractions.

Also as a reminder, here is a list of some of the exercises you were asked to do throughout the book. It will be beneficial to review these **every day** until they become second-nature:

- Notice moments when you are *waiting* for something or someone to make you happy.

- Notice when you use an object or person to *create* happiness.

- Notice how many times you complain, or feel like complaining, throughout the day.

- Notice when you have a bad feeling. It is the sign of a bad thought and/or resistance. Take a look at the thought that caused it and why it occurred.

> Notice when you relive the past or fantasize about the future.

> Know that it is not the object or person you are looking at that causes the way you feel, it is your mind.

Most of the reminders above begin with the word "notice." This is because, right now, many of us are unaware of our thoughts, feelings, beliefs, and motivations. The purpose of this book is to awaken your mind and to draw your attention to what is really going on around and within you. Many of us are currently asleep and are not fully experiencing all life has to offer. You will be amazed to find that when you shine a light on these defeating thoughts and behaviors, how quickly they disappear just because you noticed them.

Once you are fully aware of your thoughts, you will no longer need people, possessions, or ideas to make you happy. You will no longer succumb to anger, greed, jealousy, defensiveness, hatred, or stress because all of those things are caused by attachment to, and resistance of, the outside world. You must remember happiness does not come from outside sources, it comes from within.

All violent acts we witness in this world are due to feeling a loss of control and wanting the outside world to adhere to mental fantasies. Once we let go of this attachment, we will only experience joy and peacefulness.

"I will be happy once _____ happens" might be the motto for many people in this world, but now you know it doesn't have to be this way. You can be happy whenever you want to be; you just have to decide to be happy. You no longer need to chase temporary moments of happiness brought about by the outside world. Just stay under the "Joy Shower" and remain in the present moment with no complaining, resistance, reminiscing, or fantasizing, and you will be happy.

You can contemplate the past in order to learn from your mistakes, but don't dwell there. You can plan for the future, but don't become disappointed when it doesn't unfold exactly as you imagined it. You can attempt to change a situation in order to improve your life, but don't blur the lines between fantasy and reality. The only moment you can experience, and the only moment you have control over is the one you are currently experiencing. Don't overlook it because you are waiting for something better to come along.

You will not fully understand what I have tried to teach just by reading these words. Words are only concepts. You will truly understand these lessons once you find the truth within yourself. This can only happen once you have taken the time to explore your mind, feelings, and motivations, in an attempt to view the world in a new way. Think of this book as a seed, which is meant to grow a new perception of life. All I can do is hand you the seeds, it is up to you to plant them and allow them to grow within your mind and heart.

The key to lasting change is to continuously watch your thoughts and your emotions.

Watch for complaining, judgement, resistance, negative feelings, ideas of temporary fulfillment, and daydreaming of past or future.

Notice when you step outside of your "Joy Shower."

ABOUT THE AUTHOR

E.K. Christopher was born in Las Vegas, NV in 1982. The daughter of an Air Force Master Sergeant, her family, which includes her mother and older sister, moved to Crestview, FL in 1986. After graduating from high school she obtained a bachelor's degree in music from Troy University.

Following college, Ms. Christopher spent many years studying a wide-range of subjects including psychology, philosophy, eastern religions, and the categories of self-help and new age. It became her goal to find a way to bring much of her newfound knowledge into the mainstream.

E.K. Christopher currently lives in South Florida with her dog and cat, Crouton & Pickles.

www.ingramcontent.com/pod-product-compliance
Lightning Source LLC
Chambersburg PA
CBHW031502040426
42444CB00007B/1181